Smarter

Faster

Better

Work Smarter, Not Harder

to my dearest fawn eyed Noémi

you inspire me everyday

i love you

♥

Table of Contents

Dear Reader,

if you are a traditional eater and interested in how you can max out your health potential just by developing proper eating habits consider reading <u>my other book Eatin Clean</u>! This nutritional strategy helped me to get going on my still ongoing journey towards getting into and staying in the best shape of my life!

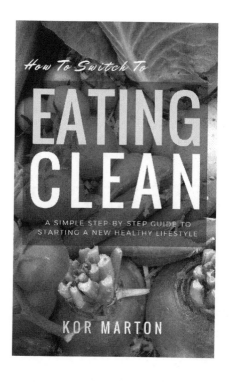

About The Author

Kor Marton is a Hungarian-born self-made polymath;
a bad boy street fighter turned legendary entrepreneur. But he is also a nutritionist, a marketer, an athlete, a life coach, a vegan activist, a teacher, an actor, a film director, a musician of many instruments and now an author but the list goes on and on.

A man of many talents is usually just a Jack of all trades and master of none. Not him. He is one of the very few exceptions. He tends to master anything he touches hence he is truly a modern age polymath.

He spent the first half of his life studying performing arts and marketing in Hungary, Europe, then the next two decades in the United States. That was where he started focusing on bettering himself in many aspects; grew a major interest in healthy nutrition, entrepreneurship, and mastering krav maga.

Today he is a successful online coach, productivity guru and major motivator for entrepreneurs. He is a huge proponent of a new way of life he calls the laptop lifestyle. He advocates online wealth creation from anywhere on the planet regardless of your nationality or geolocation. I am sure, at this moment he is doing exactly what he teaches; building his fortune on his laptop from somewhere exotic and luxurious.

His passion driven life could stand as an example to us all and a constant reminder that anything is possible, anywhere, anytime. All it takes is you, persistence and your knowledge. "We all deserve a great life filled with abundance. After all, we are all citizens of the world. That is exactly what I want to teach everyone." he claims. And he lives by his motto, too.

- Richard Bloom

Author, Seven-figure Entrepreneur

Introduction

Congratulations on purchasing *Smarter Faster Better: Work Smarter, Not Harder* and thank you for doing so. In the pages of this book, I intend to share productivity concepts and hacks I personally use on a daily basis but many people still consider as secrets. Many hard-working individuals dream of a life of success, but lack the knowledge that will help them make the most of their limited hours. Successful people utilize lesser-known methods and tactics in combinations to increase their productivity levels and work smarter, faster, and better.

The following chapters will discuss suggestions and techniques for getting tasks done at a more efficient pace with time and energy to spare. In chapter 1, readers will discover valuable hacks designed to help them get the most return out of their efforts. Chapter 2 outlines secrets that successful people use to finish their to-dos at a faster pace than the rest of the world. Chapter 3 details methods of improving one's overall performance at work, school, and other achievement-oriented institutions. The common productivity mistakes that people often make and strategies for overcoming them line the pages of chapter 4. Chapter 5 suggests useful apps and software that enable users to do more with their time. Lastly, chapter 6 includes tips that will help readers prepare for their near future; preparation breeds success.

Once again, these are not the only productivity hacks or strategies in existence. They only happen to be my personal favorite ones that I use day in, day out. They have been helping me in becoming a successful entrepreneur and I am confident they will do the same for you - if applied properly!

There are plenty of books on this subject on the market. I thank you again for choosing this one! Every effort was made to ensure it is full of as much useful information as possible. Please enjoy!

Prerequisites: Attitude & Mindset

Before we begin it is important to clear up a few things. Just to avoid misunderstandings, I will assume you have at least a basic knowledge about the proper mindset, attitude and general approach you need in order to reach your full productive potential, thus rocketing you to the zenith of your success. Without these, some of my tips, hacks, and tricks may fall flat and will yield no tangible results or simply make no sense. I will still try to explain to you my rendition of mindset, approach and general attitude that I have which has worked for me time after time, repeatedly. These three things are vital for you to understand and even master if you want to get the most out of your time and efforts with the least amount of hassle.

Attitude

According to most dictionaries *attitude is a settled way of thinking or feeling about someone or something, typically one that is reflected in a person's behavior.* I know, it also has another, informal meaning: *truculent or uncooperative behavior; a resentful or antagonistic manner.* So I hope you won't give me attitude while I talk about the proper attitude that is one of the prerequisites of being successful!

My definition of attitude is a mental state which is responsible for the inner strength in your mindset. It is usually the result of thoughts and feelings that are based on your beliefs. Attitude doesn't just build up your mindset; the quality of it is responsible for how quickly you will recover from difficult times. If your attitude is good and solid your mindset will be strong too and you will bounce back from pretty much any hard situation in a very short amount of time. In other words, with the right attitude, you will be able to stay standing even amidst the greatest storms and possibly turn disadvantages to your advantages. To put it in even simpler terms: if you can maintain a good attitude nothing can hold you back from achieving what you want.

You have probably heard the saying that you cannot control others but you can control yourself. This wisdom basically outlines that everything begins with you; be it your success or your failure. So yes, your outlook on things can cut you both ways; your perception of your possible success or failure may play a huge role in predetermining the ultimate outcome and the quality of your career. But thankfully, you are in charge and you get to decide how you set your attitude.

This is how it works: Your beliefs inform your thoughts and feelings. They inform your attitude, your attitude informs your mindset which will predetermine your approach towards your actions. And I am sure you already guessed it: when you take action based on your beliefs it is almost guaranteed that you will be successful. So lastly, your results will reinforce your beliefs and the whole cycle starts all over again.

Here is a very simple chart outlining the very simple inevitability of success (or failure, depending on your attitude) this cycle brings you:

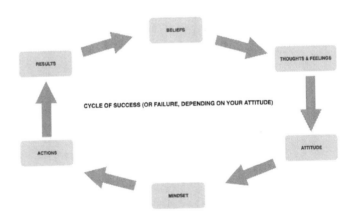

CYCLE OF SUCCESS (OR FAILURE, DEPENDING ON YOUR ATTITUDE)

Since setting your attitude is completely your choice you also get to enhance it positively if you wish. Here are a few basic ways how you can do it:

1. Be Your Own Coach

Push yourself the way a good coach would push you! Always think highly of yourself, your capabilities and your financial gains because the assessment of your ability to succeed will most likely be what you actively live out! Remember: your beliefs about yourself ultimately predetermine your results.

If you want to change the world around you start bending your reality inside you. Learn to coach yourself to manage your beliefs and with those control your thoughts and feelings. Loose the negative, defeatist, fearful patterns and charge yourself with conviction, power, and faith. A productive mindset will most likely lead to a forward momentum. This is how the quality of your attitude will ultimately determine your success or failure.

2. Motivate Yourself with Incentives

Find out what will make you spring into action! Your overall WHY is extremely important. Knowing why you do what you do will not just elevate your outlook on life, business and shift your attitude to a positive one but also will start changing people's perception about you because you will walk taller, radiate self-confidence, appear strong and friendly so you attract even more of the good stuff. If your WHY is something that will make you want to overcome even the impossible you will surely be unstoppable. Your WHY will be your everyday fuel on your journey towards success. So choose it wisely.

Your WHY is technically an overall incentive. But you can also <u>motivate yourself on a smaller scale</u> <u>by setting smaller incentives for achieving short-term goals.</u> For example, you can reward yourself for reaching a milestone in business by buying a nice car or take your co-workers out to dinner at a fancy place they have all been wanting to go once your team hits a certain number of sales. Make sure your incentives measure up and are in proportion to the goals you attempt to reach.

— PAY off HOME — GET TRUCK or TRIP...

3. Set Your Own Standard of Success

The meaning of success is different for everyone. For some it is wealth for some it is the bragging rights for some others it is helping people. Therefore it is vital to imagine and visualize your own version of success. In order to stay enthusiastic, you should constantly think about it intentionally. When you do this you will reprogram your brain. The more deeply you believe that your goal will come to pass the more likely it will actually happen. It is but natural that we all strive towards what we visualize.

4. Manage Your Fear

Most of us lose control over our thoughts and feelings when we face challenges. It is crucial to stay positive and steer clear of fear in difficult times. Discipline your thoughts to stop playing the catastrophic mind-movies of "what if". These destructively low-frequency thoughts can trigger anxiety or even panic. A forceful, constant reminder is your best antidote: remember, these slippery slope mind-movies are just stories, fabrications of your mind and they are not happening. Keep a positive attitude by focusing on things you can control; zoom in on solutions, not problems.

5. Be A Positive Character

High energy, determination and being firm is key if you want to climb to success and reach your peak potential. If you also want people to want to be around you and like to work with you, you will want to be likable. As a matter of fact, the more people like you the more successful you will become. It is not a popularity contest, but your personal vibe can push people away or attract them to you.

When your attitude is full of excitement and enthusiasm it will rub off on people around you. This will not just increase the overall morale but you will appear to them as having unlimited potential which is the best way to positively motivate others to support you in achieving even more success.

6. Stay Hungry

Don't just be hungry - stay hungry for success! Your long-term hunger will imbue your attitude and you will reek of eagerness. Put your hunger to work and use it as your emotional fuel. This will drive your efforts of attaining your goals. A 100% commitment will cut through doubt.

7. Find Your Higher Life Purpose

You can impact other's lives in a grand way by just doing what you do. This gives you the opportunity to realize that you can serve a life purpose that is way bigger than you - call it a higher meaning or a true calling. Once you have this revelation it will nourish you spiritually, empower you psychologically and ultimately be expressed through your work. Seeing how helpful and powerful your purpose is in other's lives will further strengthen you to continue doing what you do.

8. Be Lighthearted

Surround yourself with lightheartedness! Did you know humor decreases your stress? With less stress, you will have more positive energy to support your endeavors for success. When you are lighthearted, people will find you more attractive, charismatic, they will trust you more and will want to work with you or for you.

9. Be Physically Active

If some negativity got you down the best way to escape it is to start moving! Physical activity will quickly change your biochemistry thus shifting your mood and helping you gain a positive attitude. Any negative thought pattern can be interrupted by simply exercising because it will redirect your focus and energy to start seeing the positive side of things.

Technically any physical activity that will make you sweat has the potential to get you in an altered state of mind in which your optimism naturally increases. Exercising regularly is a great way to stay motivated, achieve mental clarity and release your stress naturally.

10. Master Yourself

You can only control two things: your thoughts and your feelings. Learn to control them in order to shape an invincible attitude! Master your inner world so that you can dominate the actual outer world! So consciously choose a positive attitude. It is not just recommended, it is vital. Mostly if you have pessimistic tendencies. But it is also important in order to take deliberate responsibility for your career. Talent, education, finances, resources or connections do take a huge role in reaching success but all things being equal, the only thing that will set you apart from the rest is your attitude. Choosing your attitude is entirely within your control so make it a great one! This will give you an almost unfair edge because your resilience and determination will be second to none.

As you can see, attitude is everything. If you believe you can succeed you most likely will. Create your own self-fulfilling prophesy by building a solid positive attitude. Choose to be a winner!

Mindset

Let's unpack this! According to most dictionaries mindset is the established set of attitudes held by someone. In more depth: mindset is a collection of ideas which create and shape the way you think about yourself and the world around you. It determines how you respond to challenges or setbacks. In general, we distinguish two different types of mindsets: fixed and growth mindset.

You are probably familiar with the expressions "glass-half-full/glass-half-empty". When looking at a glass that is only filled up to halfway you can either say the glass is half-full or the glass is half-empty. These refer to the same thing: your mindset. The way you process and perceive the stimuli of your surrounding. If you are more of a glass half-full person you most likely have a positive mindset and an optimistic outlook on life. and do things in a very positive way. On the other hand, if you are a glass-half-empty type, you probably have a negative mindset so you approach and think about most things in a defeatist, cynical way.

You might have guessed it: the positive mindset is the growth mindset and the negative one is the fixed one.

A person with a growth mindset is likely to:

- Want to learn from everyone

- Understand that success is the result of necessary action

- Recognize that making mistakes is an opportunity to learn

- Be aware of their own capabilities and limitations, and focused on improving their weak points

- Love challenges

- Have an open mind to new things and new ways of bettering themselves.

The opposite of this is a fixed mindset. A person with a fixed mindset is very likely to:

- Stay away from challenges

- Not being able to handle setbacks

- Try to cover up their mistakes (usually by finding excuses)

- Be convinced that their abilities are limited to one area. For example, believing that they're a 'creative' type or an 'athletic' type etc

- Talk and think in a negative, defeatist pattern by saying/thinking things like "I can't do it."

Self-limiting Beliefs

Self-limiting beliefs are the number one suspects if one generally has a growth mindset yet doesn't reach their goal. It is too common to hear excuses instead of the actual reasons of failure, retrospectively, when an undertaking goes awry. Learning from mistakes is paramount in order to grow and being able to avoid making the same errors twice. The difference between excuses and reasons of failure is often self-limiting beliefs. Unfortunately, in most cases self-limiting beliefs get in the way a lot sooner and failure happens even before taking an idea off the ground. In other words: our business may be born dead even with a growth mindset just because of what we believe of our certain capabilities.

Most of our struggles in life comes from our self-limiting beliefs. Sometimes we feel stuck but not because somebody is holding us back; we hold ourselves back. It can happen on various levels but the result can be just as bad in each case. Having a growth mindset but also having one or two self-limiting beliefs about key capabilities or qualities will hamper your success just as badly as having a completely fixed mindset. The difference is only in the areas affected. By the way, these self-limiting beliefs build a fixed mindset and you can actually spot them rather easily. Every sentence you tell yourself which starts with "I don't" or "I can't" is a self-limiting belief.

- I don't have motivation.

- I don't have time.

- I don't have enough resources.

- I don't have a clue who I am.

- I don't know where to start.

- I can't do it.

- I can't focus.

- I can't change.

Let's say your five-year-old kid goes to you and tells you in great details how he will be a famous astronaut when he grows up. Would you look him dead in the eye and say, "You want to be an astronaut? Are you kidding me? You? An astronaut? An astronaut has to be physically, mentally and psychologically in top notch shape but you are weak, dyslexic and cry easily so you really don't have what it takes to be an astronaut. So yeah, right, dream on, kid!" Would you really say it to a five-year-old? Of course, you wouldn't! You would summon up endless enthusiasm and start immersing your kid in the wonderful world of astronomy and other space sciences. Maybe even head down to your local bookstore and get an encyclopedia on planets or astronauts.

So why would we do the right thing to a five-year-old but do the worst thing to ourselves? Somewhere between childhood and adulthood, we start suppressing our natural predisposition to daring to dream and do big things. This turns us from invincible kids into scared adults impeded by our own self-limiting beliefs which flatten our self-esteem, hurt productivity and dampen success.

Can we get rid of them? Absolutely! How? It only takes three steps but they may look easier than they actually are.

1. Recognize the Problem

They say a problem well understood is a problem half solved. Recognize that you have a problem and you need to get out of your own way. While the only way to move forward is to give yourself way, recognition comes first but is not always simple. Most self-doubters have a blind spot about their self-limiting beliefs and they don't even know that they are actually their own worst enemies. In some cases, they perpetually seek approval or permission from outside sources and stall their own progress by trying to get another degree, qualification or certification. In simpler cases, it is a lot easier to spot yourself as a self-doubter; you tend to answer sensitive questions regarding your progress or goals with the "yes, but..." structure. "Were you able to make money

on that project you have been working on?"
"Well, I would have but..."

2. Reprogram Your Mind

Start with the obvious: build a brand new, solid, positive attitude. Replace your negative thought patterns with brave, high-frequency can-do beliefs. You can achieve this by regularly doing rituals, meditations, self-hypnosis, mind control and anything else that works for you in reprogramming your mind.

3. Get Out of Your Own Way

Reading positive quotes, posting famous people's positive advice on your social timeline or collecting fridge magnets with the same content may be beneficial psychologically but on their own, will not get you anywhere. If you really want to get out of your own way you will actually need to move because motion beats meditation! Take action! DO SOMETHING! Anything that will set you in motion. An object in motion tends to stay in motion - so do just that!

IF You HAVE HAD SomETHING ON
YOUR LAST - JUST DAST!

Chapter 1: Work Smarter

Hard work pays. Smart work pays, too. It also takes less energy out of you. If you learn to work smarter, you can achieve the same results with less effort and energy. Hard work will do you wonders, but it will drain your liveliness. There is absolutely nothing wrong with working hard. However, a problem is present when you work harder than you need to. In other words, if you can accomplish a task in less time by working smarter, then you should smarten up your work routine. This chapter will show you how.

To-Do List

Chances are, AT some point during your education, you heard the mantra that writing things down makes you more likely to remember them later. This is especially true of tasks, assignments, and chores. Your list of to-dos should be a physical, tangible list. When you write your to-do list down, you will stay focused and on-task. Before we talk about how to go about creating and following a to-do list, you should first understand its importance.

Why should you utilize a to-do list? It will make you more organized, motivated, and productive. It will also cause you to be less forgetful. The to-do list has made itself a mainstay in the arsenal of many successful people around the world because of its effectiveness and simplicity.

First, to-do lists help with organization. People often feel overwhelmed because they think that they have an unmanageable workload to overcome. Thankfully, when you put all of your tasks to be accomplished in a readable list, they seem a lot less intimidating. A to-do list quantifies your workload. You get to see a layout of everything that you need to get done. Furthermore, when you complete an item on your to-do list, you get to cross it off. This simple action of crossing out finished tasks will affirm your progress. If you ever doubt the sufficiency of your effort, look back at all the tasks that you crossed off and realize that you are, in fact, progressing.

Second, to-do lists benefit their users in that they assist with motivation. You can say that you want a clean apartment all you want. However, if you write down the steps that you must take in order to achieve a tidy dwelling, like sweeping and vacuuming, then you have a series of smaller goals in front of you. You will believe in your ability to get a clean apartment when you break that task down into a list of unintimidating chores. As you go about crossing items off of your list, your confidence will increase. Some people do not clean because they do not believe that they are capable of keeping an apartment clean. Those folks just need somebody to show them the steps that they have to take to achieve their goals. The next time you find yourself dwelling on a seemingly insurmountable task, ask yourself if you can get it done in a series of easy projects that all contribute towards the ultimate goal.

Third, a to-do list will breed an increase in productivity. To-do lists help us plan our work. Studies show that spending a small amount of time planning can save a huge quantity of time spent working. With a visible layout of your responsibilities, you can make informed decisions regarding which tasks you will prioritize. For example, you might always put picking up the kids from their school before making the bed. Additionally, you might notice that you can cut down on travel time. For example, your to-do list might reveal that you have to run two errands in the same shopping center. Be more efficient by finishing those errands in the same trip.

Fourth, to-do lists make us less forgetful. You do not have to mentally keep track of all of your responsibilities if you write them down together. If you ever forget what all you need to do, you can refer to your list. Additionally, you can always add items to your to-do list as you think of them. To-do lists provide a permanent reference to our responsibilities.

So, to-do lists assist people who use them with organization, motivation, productivity, and memory. Creating and using one of these beneficial tools is simple. You do not need to obtain any fancy or expensive materials. The making of a to-do list only requires a writing surface and a writing utensil. The writing surface can be something as frugal as an index card or piece of scrap paper. You need to write down what you hope to accomplish throughout the day, and then set out to complete the items on your list. Keep it in your pocket as you move locations.

What about the electronic versions of to-do list? Do they work? Certainly! Although, in my opinion, it also depends on the person who uses them. I, for one, love technology and enjoy how it can multiply my efforts and speed up a lot of things I have to do yet I do a lot better with an "old school", handwritten to-do list on paper. For me, that is the only thing I always like to do tangibly.

There is another interesting thing about handwritten notes. Recent studies indicate that there might be more than just a motoric connection between your writing hand and your brain. The most powerful part of your mind is undoubtedly your subconscious. It is responsible for the things you attract by way of your beliefs, drive and other factors of your determination. Your subconscious does all the heavy lifting in the background and it feeds off of mostly emotions and visuals. In other words, your subconscious doesn't understand words. If you want to communicate with it or even program it you need to rely on images you see and feelings you feel. Writing with your hands is both a visual and an emotional experience. The same thing does not seem to be fully true about typing.

Do THIS!

One Thing at a Time

Credible, peer-reviewed studies suggest that the most productive people are those who can focus in on one task at a time. You might get tempted to have multiple projects going at one time, especially if you feel overwhelmed. However, the most productive way of working involves steadily tackling individual tasks one after the other. For example, imagine that you are a full-time university student. You have to read a chapter and write a paper before class tomorrow. If you have the reading and the writing both simultaneously open on your computer, switching between them at will, then you will not be fully focused on either. Tackling one assignment at a time will allow you to give your schoolwork the attention that it deserves and requires.

How do you want to do it.

Give off Busy Signals

Sometimes, you just have to shut out the outside world while you attempt to get things done on time. You can inform others of your desire to work undisturbed. Most online chat platforms let users display some sort of a "do not disturb" status next to their names. Something as simple as closing the door to your office will prevent pesky coworkers from popping in to distract you. If you cannot shut yourself into an isolated work environment, you can still give your office mates the idea that you are trying to focus and wish not to be disturbed. For example, consider putting on a pair of earbuds and intently working on your most pressing project. The combination of focused working and something to block out outside noises will signal that you are too busy to attend to other people's trivial matters.

A brilliant real life example of this in a fairly recent story. A famous Silicon Valley entrepreneur, whom I will not name here, wanted to invite his billionaire friend Richard Branson to speak at one of his events. They were not just acquaintances but indeed, good friends. As a matter of fact, our Silicon Valley friend had Mr. Branson's personal cell phone number on speed dial yet he couldn't get a hold of him for days. Eventually, he was able to speak with Mr. Branson's personal assistant who told him that he was under strict orders from Mr. Branson to turn everyone away including close family and friends because Mr. Branson has been working on his next project

Doesn't work for me - just hard to focus need door note

which required his undivided focus for the following two days.

Feel Free to Say No

At times, your plate gets full and stays that way. When this happens, handle your business before you take on more responsibility. If you cannot complete another person's request, tell them that you are too busy. Do not let other people pressure you into complying with their request. Kindly inform the requester that you are currently busy with other projects. You may even list out those projects for them if you feel comfortable with it.

Find Your Golden Hours

7-10 AM For ME

Most humans are most productive at a certain two-hour interval during the day. The specific timeframe of the golden hours' interval varies from person to person. For most working people, those hours take place in the morning, immediately after they wake up. Sadly, many people waste those hours easing into their day, perhaps watching television or browsing social media. You should instead take advantage of your natural tendency to be productive at certain hours. Save your leisure activities for times when you feel drained and unproductive.

Although the Rule of the Golden Hours is true regardless of the kind of work you do, it may be extremely of your service if you do creative work. Among many other things, I am an author so I write. Writer's block is no stranger to me either. It has already happened to me several times yet I didn't let it stop me from being productive. The only way I was able to overcome this paralyzing brain cramp was to force myself to work on an empty stomach directly after waking up, in my Golden Hours. As a healthy lifestyle advocate and a nutritionist, I would tell you to either eat or work out within the first 30 to 60 minutes after waking up. This will get your metabolism cranking which is super healthy! But if your Golden Hours are similar to mine and fall exactly after waking up then I recommend doing the second best thing; rinse your mouth with clean water then start drinking water or green tea right away! (Please note, I didn't say coffee or black tea! They have their place and time but it is not here and now.)

One Touch, One Task

People's houses get messy because they set things down without ever revisiting them. As a result, items become out of place, unwashed, and generally out of order. So, as soon as you touch something in your home or office, take care of it right away. Throw away packaging as soon as you open its contents. Wash dishes as soon as you are done eating. Make your bed immediately after you are done sleeping. At the office, reply to an email as soon as you read it; delete every unneeded email. If the phone rings, answer it if doing so will not interrupt an important conversation. By leaving nothing for later, you stand to catch up sooner.

Set Time Aside for Emails

One of the modern office's biggest stressors is one's own email inbox. Emails can come in at any time of the day. When you are constantly reading emails as you get them, you can get stressed out and lose focus of the task at hand. Furthermore, some people constantly check their email out of fear of missing an important one or reading it too late. Instead, what you should do is devote a portion of your day to nothing but handling work emails. At this time, you can give the emails in your inbox the attention that they require.

Perhaps you are worried that a sender of an email of yours may think that you are purposefully ignoring them when you fail to open their email for hours. Fear not, however; just leverage on technology to make your life easier! With most mail clients you can establish an automatic response to emails that you receive at certain hours of the day. You choose the hours during which this automatically generated reply will go out to senders. In these response emails, you can inform your senders that you will only be tending to emails at certain predetermined times during the day.

In addition, you might worry about missing a time-sensitive email if you implement this productivity strategy. Fortunately, you can use programs that send alerts to your phone and desktop when you receive emails from certain people of your choice. In addition, you can choose to receive alerts when senders deem that their messages contain a high level of priority.

Directly Deposit Payments

Direct deposit is a program that most modern Western banks offer its customers at no charge. When you set up your paychecks for direct deposit, your employer will deposit your pay right into your bank account. You will receive exactly the same sum of money that you would have if you had opted to received a check. However, you do not need to visit a bank in order to get your money into your account. A direct deposit program can save you hundreds, if not thousands, of trips to the bank in your lifetime. Ask your employer about their direct deposit policies. Most reputable organizations require that you only fill out and turn in a form in order to establish a direct deposit system for yourself.

The same is true if you are your own employer because you are self-employed. I highly recommend leveraging on modern technology. Pick a bank which offers on-line banking with a lot of features. The basic actions (like on-line bill pay, invoicing, etc.) are usually free or provided for a very low fee.

Plan Your Day According to a Theme

Real life is multifaceted and should be treated as such. If you dedicate too much focus to one aspect of your life, you have to sacrifice the attention that would have otherwise been given to another. For example, if you spend more time on your schoolwork, that leaves you with less time to clean your apartment. Resolve this tension by planning each day according to a theme. For example, if you are a college student, the first half of your week might look like this:

- *Sunday: Schoolwork.*
  Spend all of your working hours finishing up the majority of your coursework. Not only is this productive, but it also sets you up to smoothly glide through the school week and focus on other tasks without worrying about whether you will finish an assignment by the time it is due. Spend the day reading assigned texts, writing papers, and completing homework.

- *Monday: Money.*
  Of course, if you are like most college students, you will have to attend classes and possibly work a day job on Mondays. However, you can still accomplish a lot during your breaks and time after class and work. You might use this day to tend to financial matters. Transfer money from your PayPal account to your checking account; plan out your budget for the near future; figure out how many hours you have to work to stay out of debt; pay the utility bill; deposit your paycheck, for example.

- *Tuesday: Tidying Up.*
  In addition to your scheduled obligations, you might use this day to get caught up on cleaning. Take the time to tidy up your home and catch up on household chores like laundry and lingering dishes.

- *Wednesday: Working.*
  When I was a college kid, I took on a part-time job. The hours were flexible and I felt fortunate that I could decide when I wanted to work so I picked Wednesday - oh, and not just for the alliteration! I made every attempt to make a little extra income every day. However, I would dedicate one day a week to nothing but working on my second job. If you have a freelance job that lets you set your own hours, consider spending the majority of one day

every week to finishing projects for that job and you will start seeing an unstoppable progress!

If you are no longer in college and, say, you are an entrepreneur your week may look very similar to mine, just like this:

- *Sunday: Scheduling.*
  Normally I don't work on the weekends. Family deserves some exclusive quality time. After Sunday brunches or lunches I still take some quiet time with my calendar and schedule out my upcoming week. Interestingly, this only takes a very short time yet it seems to be one of the most crucial tasks in order to make the most of my time every week.
  Call me old fashioned but I also happen to like to do some of my own maintenance work around my house. A busted light bulb? Do leaves need raking in the backyard? A door hinge must be adjusted? No problem! Your hobby handyman-gardener is already on it!

- *Monday: Money.*
  This one hasn't changed for me over the years. I pay bills, do my banking, check on my investments and income streams, talk to my tax attorney and do everything money related you can possibly imagine. I usually do a week-to-week comparison to

keep my finger on the pulse and see how I am doing financially compared the previous weeks and my plans. Besides, what can be a better start for the week than looking at your finances? If you have a lot of money or a positive revenue - that's why! It will fuel your hunger for more and boost your morale for the rest of the week! If you don't have a lot of money or not much money coming in - that's why! Use the frustration you may feel as fuel to want to achieve more! Great things come from places of desperation! And if you think it's commonsense that Mondays are grim and terrible no matter what maybe you should stop reading those silly Garfield comics.

Let's make Mondays great!

- *Tuesday: Tackling Tasks.*
  Tuesday is where I do most of my heavy lifting. Similarly to my college years, I tidy up, but this time it is not my apartment. It is my business I take care of. I tackle tasks that are overdo or otherwise urgent. This is also the day when I delegate. As a new age entrepreneur I leverage on technology and people who work for me so I delegate to both humans and machines. They are my multipliers. They allow me to be more effective thus achieveing more in a shorter period of time.

- *Wednesday: Working & Writing.*
  I outsource some of the workload, mostly the repetitive or monotonous tasks, but there is still that personal element only I can put in. This is when I actually work. In the past few months, it has been writing but this is also when I do my Youtube videos although lately, I try to cram out a video in my coffee breaks on some other days as well.

- *Thursday: Teaching.*
  I coach on Thursdays. All day. It is a great opportunity for me to connect with real live people and share what I know via Facetime, FB video chat or Skype. Thursdays are precious and personal for me.

- *Friday: Follow Up.*
  When you delegate you will also want to follow up. I usually fill my Fridays with follow up calls and reading, writing follow-up emails. Anyone working for me knows this and they email me their status report prior to Friday, which is usually Thursday night so that I can read it and respond to it on Friday, if necessary.

- *Saturday: Social.*
  This is not really about work. Or not necessarily. Time to relax a bit and enjoy life with the ones you love. Family and friends. During the day I also like to turn my fitness activities into social happenings. This includes going for a 2-3 hour

hike with family, rollerskate or play tennis with them or drag my friends to a nearby dojo to do some ju jitsu ground fighting.
Active and social during the day and maybe a party in the evening.

Of course, these are just examples of themes that you can apply to the days that you have been blessed with. Choose daily themes that work for you and your lifestyle. Handle any urgent situations as they arise. Giving a theme to each day will help prevent you from engaging in unproductive multitasking, as well as give your day focus and direction.

Wake Up!

Several super successful CEOs say that waking up and removing oneself from bed early is an essential factor of their success. Naturally, when you wake up earlier, you have more hours of daylight to work with. Additionally, waking up before your peers do gives you more free time to enjoy. When we start our workday, we tend to focus on work and not much else for the remainder of the day. Sadly, thinking about work all the time can make one feel exhausted. Fortunately, if you wake up earlier, you can spend some time doing enjoyable activities before you start grinding out tasks. Many people who like to wake up at very early hours do not usually spend the first hours of their day working. Instead, they take care of their personal well-beings. Happy early risers use their morning free time to exercise, meditate, read for leisure, and indulge in other relaxing activities. The relaxation that early risers enjoy before work enhances their mood and therefore leads to a more productive workday. Get up before your competition, even if that competition is yourself.

I tend to ~~~~ wake up early. This truly gives me more daylight to work with, makes me feel that I am ahead of the curb but most importantly it gives me extra time to do my morning rituals. These are not religious rituals although I do them religiously. It takes me about 30-40 minutes to "get right with myself" every morning. This is when I meditate and eliminate all distractive feelings that can jeopardize my productivity. Feelings with low-frequency vibrations like fear, hate, anger, jealousy, vengeance and their likes must go. If you let them stay in your head, in your heart they will not allow you to focus and get the most of your day. You might have guessed it already, it is forgiveness that I seek. I forgive to everyone who ever wronged me and ask for forgiveness from the ones I might have hurt. Yes, I do this out of selfish reasons just for myself so that I can reach my full potential yet the outcome truly benefits everyone.

Do the Dreaded Before the Tolerable

Have you been putting off an important task because you know that completing it will require nearly all of your effort and energy? If so, start that project immediately. When you put off a lingering, yet somewhat urgent task or assignment, you let it hover over your head until you actually do it. When you tackle dreaded, undesirable tasks first, you feel a huge sense of accomplishment before you even finish your workload. The rest of your to-dos will seem easy in comparison. This sensation will motivate you and make you more productive. Stop putting off dreaded yet important projects. Handling them first will make you happier and contribute to a better performance when it comes to the rest of your to-do list.

Tackle Two-Minute To-Dos

Some chores and tasks can be completed in a matter of two minutes or fewer. Get yourself ahead of schedule by immediately doing all tasks, projects, and assignments that require no more than two minutes of your time. Immediately attending to these miniscule chores will prevent them from piling up. A two-minute to-do may not seem like much to put off, but, over time, they can add up if left unattended. For example, for those who are relatively tidy, making the bed and tidying up the bedroom each require about two minutes of time. Still, many people put these tasks off until later in the day, telling themselves that they have to get out the door as soon as possible.

Similarly, some individuals have trouble staying on top of their dishes, especially if their household lacks a dishwashing machine. Truthfully, in most cases, washing a set of dishes used to prepare and consume a simple meal takes about two minutes. Somehow, some people fail to do their dishes in a timely manner. As a result, dishes pile up, the person responsible for them gets overwhelmed, and the kitchen sink looks messy. If you do your dishes right after you are done eating, you can save yourself a hassle in the form of a huge stack of unwashed dishes.

You must Learn To Do Dishes!

The other benefit of tackling two-minute to-dos first is psychological. If you get something done quickly however easy or mundane it is, you will still have a sweeping sense of accomplishment. The visual confirmation of crossing out one or more items on your to-do list in a short time might also give you wings for the rest of your tasks. If you need to do a chore, and you can do it in under two minutes, do it now, immediately.

Get Away from Your Desk

Studies show that humans perform optimally when they get to work in a variety of locations and settings. Therefore, sitting at your desk all day will put a strain on your productivity. Try exposing yourself to a variety of locations throughout your workday. This is not to say that you should leave your desk in order to avoid working, however. Instead, see if you can get work done from other places; your smartphone will greatly assist with this. For example, reply to emails from the bench in front of your building. Make a phone call while you take a stroll. If your company allows it, spend an hour or two working from your laptop in a nearby coffee shop. When you go back to your desk, you will feel invigorated from the change of scenery and the exercise that you performed in order to experience it.

Flex Time!

I AGREE

If your company has a strict policy regarding the locations from which you can work, see if you can use this tactic within the confines of your workplace. Can you move to an unoccupied desk for a portion of the day? Maybe you can get away with working from the break room for an hour.

If you are your own boss try to create a fun working environment for yourself and your working peers. Interior design, your choice of furniture and potted plants, the color of your walls and even the amount of stuff on your shelves can all be important contributing factors. You should feel joy and happiness when you work.

Important: don't make it distractive but fun! The idea behind it is to connect productivity and ultimately your success with feeling joyful. This concept will help you want to achieve more even after you are no longer "hungry".

In any case, a change of perspective will greatly increase your productivity levels.

Make a List of Don'ts

While to-do lists are used to outline everything that one hopes to accomplish in a given timespan, a to-don't list can be just as beneficial. Mostly for beginners. Write down everything that is preventing you from being productive. Include things like browsing social media, watching television, and playing computer games. These activities, in most cases, add nothing to the quality of one's life and serve only to minimize productivity. Make a list of your biggest time-wasters and vow to only engage in them when you have no items left on your to-do list, if at all.

Chapter 2: Finish Faster

Sometimes, you just have to work hard. No amount of technology or mind-bending will make your task any easier. In these cases, you will want to learn some tips for doing the same amount of work with the same level of quality in less time.

Disconnect

If you have to get something done quickly, minimize your digital distractions. Power down your cell phone. Sign out of all of your social media and email accounts. (Of course, if you need a certain device or platform to accomplish your task, then connect with it). By cutting out unneeded distractions, you stand to devote more focus to your prioritized work.

Many writers who work to meet deadlines will use this tactic to finish projects in time. Writers have an unconventional work schedule in that they set their own hours and get paid according to their productivity level, either by the word or by the task. As such, they must complete work on their own time. They do not clock in and out like traditional day jobs require. So, when writers need to write a large amount of words in a short span of time, they like to disconnect from the outside world and focus in on their work.

Of course, emergencies can happen. Few things in life are worse than needing to get ahold of someone while they cannot be reached. As such, experts recommend having one person whom you trust screen your connections for emergencies. Then, they can inform you if something truly more pressing than your high-priority work needs your attention.

Make Your Mouse Move Faster

This one may seem funny at first or even downright silly but it has worked for me! Today's home and office computers give users the ability to adjust the speeds at which their mouse cursors move. If you have to complete a task on your computer that involves moving the mouse at all, you can save precious seconds by cranking up your cursor's speed. Try doubling its speed now. You might have trouble getting used to the increase in speed for a day or so. However, this adjustment period is worth suffering through. Once you can move your cursor about your screen with speed and ease, you will get computer work done much faster than you had before. Go into your computer's settings and adjust your mouse's speed.

Set Time Limit Deadlines

Studies and theories suggest that if you have a long time to finish a task, then it will take you a long time to finish it. On the other hand, if you have a highly limited time, then you will, in all likelihood, finish that project in near record time. Humans tend to spend as much time working on things as they are allowed. Hey, if you are working for two hours, even if you work slowly, then you still feel productive. However, feeling productive and actually being productive are not necessarily two sides of the same coin.

To manipulate this psychological phenomenon, you should set time limits for yourself. For example, utilize a stopwatch and try to finish replying to all of your emails for the day in thirty minutes. Go crazy trying to finish a multiple-page report in two hours. You will naturally work faster as you try to defeat the clock.

In addition, the increase in your levels of effectiveness and productivity will make you feel accomplished, happier, and thus more motivated to continue working hard. Your brain will reward you with happiness when you finish important tasks that ultimately contribute towards your continued survival. You will then chase that feeling of happiness, leading to even more increases in productivity.

You can use almost anything as a timer for this tactic. As mentioned earlier, a stopwatch will do. In addition, the clock on your wall or computer will give you something to race against. You can even challenge yourself to finish a project before the shadow on your desk reaches a certain point. Or, maybe you just want to complete a paper before the cafeteria stops serving lunch. In any case, setting short deadlines for yourself will help you finish work faster.

Pretend Your Workday is Two Hours Long

What do you usually do during your first two hours at work? You plan on being there for eight hours, so you might as well enjoy your morning. Perhaps you sip coffee, check messages, and briefly talk with co-workers. Instead, try plowing through your workload in the first two hours. If you start at 9:00 A.M., imagine that you have to go home at 11:00 A.M. Complete consequential projects. Make a list of the most pressing tasks that you find yourself faced with and start working on them. This tactic will force you to finish the projects that matter the most. You will be surprised to discover how much you can accomplish in two hours if you pretend that you do not have more time.

Finish Menial Tasks Quickly

If your workplace often burdens you with menial, largely unimportant assignments, try to do them speedily. Put just enough effort into low-importance tasks so that they get done adequately. Save your efforts for tasks that matter more.

Some workers use menial tasks as a tool for procrastinating on daunting projects. By spending more time working on unimportant tasks, they delay their work on the inevitable yet undesirable projects that await them. Never use unimportant work to procrastinate on pressing projects. Give yourself ten minutes to power through tasks of low importance. That way, you can give the projects that truly matter the attention and energy that they deserve and require.

Consume Caffeine

Before I get into this subject I have to say a few words as a nutritionist. Caffeine has been vilified for a long time. The truth is, it is both good and bad. Just like mostly everything it has two sides. In moderation, it could be an enhancement. But consuming it for longer periods of time may create an immunity towards its effects or in greater quantities, it may even permanently harm your body. It is a scientific consensus that about 400mg per day which is about 2-4 cups of drip coffee is the tolerable amount for an average adult. If consumed responsibly and clean (no milk or cream or sugar) it has a lot of wonderful benefits. If there is anything I learned during my nearly two decades in the United Stated is that coffee is the most delicious productivity tool of all times. Yes, it is a drug, therefore, it needs to be treated with the same caution and respect as any other drug should be.

Caffeine is a great resource for those who need to accomplish menial tasks quickly. The substance assists with speed on tasks that its consumers are already familiar with. In other words, caffeine will not help you to more quickly complete a task that you are not already good at. Thankfully, though, you can use caffeine to help power through monotonous, tedious projects like household cleaning, reading, and typing up written work.

Effectively dosing your caffeine consumption will further increase the speed at which you finish tedious tasks. The secret lies in taking smaller doses at more frequent intervals. Consuming no more than one average sized cup per hour will optimize your productivity levels. Your body can only contain so much caffeine at one time. If you consume more than you can handle, your body will immediately filter it out by processes of urination, sweating, and sometimes even vomiting in the cases of copious amounts. This filtering will cause varying levels of dehydration, therefore, it is paramount that you also rehydrate yourself by drinking plenty of water when you drink coffee!

The perfect dose of caffeine will vary by individual. Experiment with various doses of caffeine until you find one that works for your lifestyle and workload.

Lastly, coffee napping is an effective way to efficiently garner rest. To perform a coffee nap, quickly drink a cup of coffee and lie down for a nap. The coffee will not immediately prevent you from sleeping. The average human body takes twenty minutes in order to metabolize caffeine. Thus, you will wake up from your coffee nap rested and further powered by a jolt of caffeine in your brain.

Create a Workspace Free of Distractions and Clutter

Sometimes, distractions prevent us from finishing the important tasks that we set out to do. Also, clutter can make it easy to misplace documents and supplies, causing you to waste time searching for them. As such, it is crucial that you eliminate as many distractions and as much clutter from your workspace as possible. For example, if you do homework at home, keep your desk surface tidy. Your surroundings will reflect on the quality of your work; if you keep a neat workspace, your work will have a better chance of coming out organized and well-produced. In addition, take care to ensure that your preferred workspace contains sufficient lighting and ventilation. Lastly, keep your workspace stocked with any supplies that you might need, such as calculators, erasers, pencil sharpeners, writing utensils, and scrap paper. A properly cultivated workspace can make a world of difference when it comes to one's productivity levels.

The same is true in regards of your virtual workspace! If you work with computers have your computer in check. Install updates, declutter your inbox, clean up your desktop, empty your trash can, regularly archive your working folders on one but preferably two external hard drives for maximum safety. I hope it goes without saying that you shouldn't be doing this during your working hours. Installing an update can take a long time and so can copying folders. This is just simple maintenance. Do it while you don't work.

Understand What is Asked of You

Many students and working people struggle to get projects finished on time because they fail to comprehend instructions. Furthermore, many teachers and college professors find themselves frustrated when students turn in an assignment that does not make any attempt to follow the assignment's directions. Before you dive head first into a project, make sure you understand what you are expected to do. Familiarize yourself with the instructions; do not go about creating work that adheres to nobody's guidelines but your own. In most cases, you will receive instructions and an accompanying set of expectations from the person who assigns you work. Understanding these instructions will allow you to work with a goal in mind, giving you direction, purpose, and a pretty good idea of how much effort you can be expected to give to a certain project.

For students, understand the assignments that your instructors give. Many college course grades depend on a small number of large assignments. For example, I took an art history class in college where the only graded assignments we turned in for the semester were three essays, two exams, and a writing assignment. Six graded assignments determined students' final grades in the class. As such, the learners in that class could ill afford to lose points for reasons related to following directions. We were expected to fulfill a certain number of requirements for each assignment.

So, if you are currently enrolled in school, make sure you read all assignment sheets and syllabi that you receive. If you are unsure of what you are expected to do on a certain assignment, ask your instructor for help or further clarification.

In addition, working professionals must understand the workloads that their bosses expect them to tackle. If you ever feel unsure of the tasks that you are responsible for at work, the best thing you can do is talk to your superior about it. Ask for a detailed outline of your responsibilities and obligations. They will be happy that you asked, as your inquiry will demonstrate that you care about doing your job well.

If you are your own boss hopefully you have a clear vision of what it is that you want to accomplish and how. In case you don't, there are several methods that can help you clarify the what and how factors. These methods are beyond the scope of this book but personal coaching can be a great way for you to go about it.

Stand Up to Distractors (Literally)

Have you ever found yourself deeply involved in your work, only to experience a distraction from one of your coworkers or peers? Of course, you should try to give these people the attention that they deserve. However, sometimes a deadline dictates that you have to keep interpersonal interactions short and concise.

The next time you need to ensure that an interaction remains as brief as possible, refuse to sit down. The other person, the distractor, will likely remain standing as well. Standing will make them uncomfortable after a short amount of time, and they will have a desire to escape that uncomfortable feeling. As such, you can get back to work and make the other person feel attended to and heard. If somebody enters your office, desk space, or workspace, stand up when you greet them and do not sit back down until your interaction is completed.

The reason that standing up makes people more likely to keep their conversations brief stems from the fact that most of our lengthy interactions take place while seated. We enjoy most of our meals while seated at a table. Meetings and business conferences take place at long tables surrounded by seats. Classrooms provide a desk and chair for each student. In Western cultures, extended activities that do not involve physical activity take place while seated.

On the other hand, the person who provides the distraction may take it upon themselves to sit down. If this happens, stay calm and keep standing. You standing while they sit will make them uncomfortable and cause them to leave sooner. Human psychology dictates that seated individuals feel inferior to those who choose to stand, assuming that both parties have a fair choice in the matter. The seated person is more vulnerable in that position in many ways.

Furthermore, the power difference created in this scenario will make the distractor uneasy as well. People with more authority stand up while others sit. Educational instructors stand and teach while students sit down and learn. Entertainers stand up and perform on stage while the audience members enjoy their own seats. By literally standing up to human distractions, you can keep interactions brief so that you might get back to more important projects.

Chapter 3: Perform Better

The human body requires careful maintenance and diligent care in order for it to perform at its best. The suggestions in this chapter are designed to help you feel fit to deliver your best efforts at all times.

Get In the Zone

I will start off this chapter with one of my personal favorites. In order to perform at your best, it is crucial to "get in the zone". You can achieve this in more than one ways but my favorite is doing what I call My Morning Ritual. This is technically my version of Vishen Lakhiani's Six Phase Meditation. The six phases are Connection, Gratitude, Freedom from negative charges, Creative visualization, Intentions for the day and Blessing. If you ever want to give it a try, do it right before you start working or better yet, this should be the first thing you do every morning as part of your work routine. This little recurring twenty-minute activity has become so important in my life that I have it on my calendar for every morning. It may or may not work for you but all I can say, it has done wonders in my life. Both in my private and my business life.

I am aware that there are many other forms of mental or spiritual exercises which will sharpen your senses, turn up your drive and eliminate your emotional distractions. If you already have something in place that works, don't change it! If not then please experiment and find that one that is right for you.

Use Multipliers

It is probably the most important tip of them all. Technically, it is the secret behind how some people can become rich in a short amount of time. Have you ever wondered how they do it? How can some people make a lot more money than others? Simple. They can get a lot more done in the same amount of time as everyone else because they use multipliers.

Financially successful people have the same twenty-four hours in their day as everyone else. Sure, they may wake up early, just to be ahead of the curb or work more than the rest but this still doesn't count for the inequalities in the amounts of money made by them or Joe Average. The difference lies in their approach. They seem to clearly understand Rockefeller's age old statement: "I would rather earn 1% off a 100 people's efforts than 100% of my own efforts." And that is the multiplier we are talking about. Pure leverage.

When successful entrepreneurs work on a money making project they build a system that will multiply their efforts for a proportionally multiplied profit. Their job is actually not the project itself but building the system that can complete and repeat completing the project over and over again. Once the system is complete and all of this can be automatically done even when the entrepreneur is not looking we are talking about passive income. This is the most common way to scale up one's income along with one's operation.

So how can you use multipliers? Create a system for your project, outsource all steps so your system can successfully run and complete multiple projects at once and in a short amount of time. Then rinse and repeat. In an automated system, there may be both human and non-human multiplier elements. Internet entrepreneurs prefer using the multiplying power of the internet and make it work for them even when they are asleep.

To explain in greater details how you could use multipliers and potentially profit from them is beyond the scope of this publication. If you want to know more you may want to download my FREE ebook about this subject here.

Sleep Well

Human evolution dictates that we need a certain amount of sleep each night in order to operate optimally. However, some factors prevent us from getting sufficient quantities of sleep. A lack of sleep often contributes to poor memory, a short lifespan, low quality of life, higher levels of inflammation, lowered creativity, poor athletic performance, depression, and poor concentration ability. Thankfully, strategies for navigating poor sleep habits exist.

First, do not keep a clock visible. If you have an illuminated clock inside of the room in which you sleep, relocate it or hide it when you sleep. The view of an accurate, working clock during resting hours can make one anxious, especially when they need to wake up by a certain time the next day. The mind races as it thinks about how unpleasant it will be trying to get by on so many hours of sleep the next day. Illuminated clocks remind troubled sleepers that they are not yet asleep, but time is still passing. If you see a clock when you are trying to sleep, you will be reminded of the fact that precious minutes are being wasted trying to fall asleep instead of being spent sleeping. An illuminated clock's presence can interfere with the quality of one's sleep.

Illuminated clocks do not belong in the bedroom. However, the question of whether an analog clock has a place in one's sleeping quarters comes down to personal preference. For some, the rhythmic ticking provides a soothing sound that helps them sleep. For others, the constantly present noise that they make interferes with sleep and reminds them of the precious minutes wasted in a restless state.

Second, avoid using technology before bed. Devices with backlit screens prevent humans from entering deep sleep if they are used before one attempts to sleep. The blue light that they emit affects the brain in such a way that inhibits slumber. Turn off and power down your computer, tablet, smartphone, and television at least one hour before you set out to fall asleep.

Third, align your spine with your hips. When these body parts are unaligned, a mild pain in the lower back usually results. While this pain may not provide much noticeable discomfort, it can still hurt the quality of one's sleep. Negate the effects that mild lower back discomfort has on sleep quality by using a pillow strategically. If you sleep on your side, sandwich a pillow between your legs. If you prefer to sleep on your back, place a soft pillow beneath the pits of your knees. By properly aligning your hips with your spine while you sleep, you will minimize the amount of lower back pain that often wakes people up, if only briefly.

Fourth, make use of noise neutralizers. Distinct sounds that stand out from the rest of the soundscape can wake up sleepers and keep awake those who wish to fall asleep. Thankfully, you can negate the wakeful effects of some of those noises. Apps and machines that generate white, pink, brown, and red noise exist. When sound comes into contact with consistent colored noise, it blends in with the colored noise. As such, wakeful noises and sounds will become indistinct, thus less likely to keep you awake. Furthermore, you can use a fan or vent to the same effect. Anything that drowns out distinct sound will help you sleep better.

Fifth, do not consume stimulating substances during the hours close to your bedtime. These include caffeine, cocaine, nicotine, and MDMA. The aforementioned drugs activate the part of the brain responsible for keeping you awake. As such, they should be avoided before bed.

A good night's rest will contribute to better levels of productivity. Studies repeatedly prove that, when all other variables are equal, a person who gets sufficient sleep will experience a better memory, a longer lifespan, a more enjoyable life, less bodily inflammation, more creativity, better athletic performances, more happiness, and a better ability to concentrate than will a person who sleeps poorly.

Eat Right

If you want to perform well in school and at your job, you have to choose to consume healthy foods. Indulging in an occasional sweet treat is okay, but you don't get used to eating junk foods. Unhealthy sweets will hamper your productivity. The human body has evolved to thrive off of certain nutritious foods. As such, you should take great care to give your body the fuel that it needs for optimal performance.

I am not going to lecture you on everything that you should and should not eat. This is not a book on proper nutrition. Instead, this section will focus on the benefits of eating right and tips for making healthy eating a regular habit. A healthy, well-rounded, wholesome diet will lead to improved brain performance.

The human body takes the foods that you feed it and turns them to glucose. Glucose is like gasoline for the brain. Without glucose, you will fail to be alert. Consequently, your ability to perform productively will diminish. Just like a car will not run well without quality gasoline, the human body and brain will not perform at their best without the right sources of glucose.

Foods high in carbohydrates and sugars give your body a quick injection of glucose that quickly diminishes. That is why when you eat a candy bar, you feel energized for a few minutes before you feel sluggish and drained. On the other hand, more wholesome carbohydrate-heavy menu items like bread and pasta give you healthier doses of quick-release glucose. If you absolutely need a quick burst of energy, opt for a meal high in carbs but low in added sugars. For example, try a bowl of pasta. As an added bonus, pasta has a simple preparation process and a small price tag.

Some other foods, however, take our bodies longer to turn to glucose. Fatty meals like cheeseburgers and French fries provide a steady stream of glucose supply. Unfortunately, our bodies have to work much harder to turn them into fuel. As a result, fatty foods keep us full longer, but require much more effort to digest. You might save a few minutes if you choose a take-out meal over a home-prepared one, but you will suffer later in the day as your body gets drained of its energy trying to turn your fatty lunch into glucose.

Because they provide such a steady stream of energy while simultaneously filling your stomach, you will crave fatty and greasy menu items when you are the most drained. As such, maintaining a healthy diet requires an element of willpower. You already know that fast foods, in most cases, do not make the best choices of meals. Still, they can be tempting and delicious. Thankfully, you can take some steps that will help you make better dining decisions throughout the workday.

First, plan your next meal before you need it. Decide on what you will eat for lunch during the time that you are still full from breakfast. Studies show that humans tend to make poorer dining choices when they are hungrier. Give yourself an edge by planning your meals at least a few hours in advance.

Second, maintain an elevated baseline level of glucose by lightly snacking throughout the day. Some sources suggest that a daily helping of six small meals is better for you than three large ones. So, keep your glucose levels up by moderately grazing on healthy snacks like fresh fruit, rice cakes, vegetables, nuts, and protein bars. You do not want your glucose levels to fall below a certain point of uncomfortableness. If your blood sugar gets too low, you stand to suffer from lower levels of self-control, willpower, motivation, and productivity.

Third, give yourself easy access to healthy foods. Convenience plays a big part in determining what one eats for lunch. A homemade dish costs much less than a drive-thru combo meal, but fast food corporations still thrive. If you make good meal choices more accessible for yourself, you will be more likely to make the right decisions regarding your dining habits. For example, keep your desk stocked with wholesome snacks. Make use of Amazon's automatic reorder feature; you can have healthy nonperishable snacks of your choosing delivered to either your office or home at regularly scheduled intervals. Also, browse the bulk section of your local supermarket. You might just find your new favorite low-cost healthy indulgence. Furthermore, consider lugging produce like apples and carrot sticks to your workplace. This small extra effort will reward you with a healthier body and increases in productivity and energy.

Eating fresh fruits and vegetables will help the brain produce the proper amounts of chemicals needed for optimal functioning. A healthy diet will not only make you more productive, but happier and more healthful as well.

Be Active

Exercise and physical activity contribute to a more productive life. In most cases, an active person will have more energy, higher levels of happiness, and a more fulfilling career than will someone who opts to live a sedentary lifestyle. Studies repeatedly suggest that exercise improves mental health, energy levels, alertness capabilities, and physical health. In other words, if you exercise regularly, you will be healthier, and thus more productive.

First, exercise breeds better mental health. Physical activity has been proven to reduce feelings of depression as well as anxiety. The serotonin that exercise causes your brain to release makes you more mentally stable. This brain chemical, serotonin, helps your brain make needed adjustments to your emotions and moods.

Second, physical exercise increases the energy levels of exercisers. By increasing your physical fitness, you wear out less easily. If your job places physical demands onto you, then getting in shape will almost certainly improve your performance at work. In addition, physically fit people have a lower risk of hurting themselves while performing their jobs.

Third, regular physical activity will help you to be more alert, more often. Blood flows to the brain more rapidly during periods of physical exertion. The resulting consequences are increased levels of awareness and alertness.

Fourth, exercise leads to better physical health. You will miss less days at work due to illness if you are physically fit. You will become less likely to develop serious illnesses. In return, you will experience high levels of endurance that will help you fulfill your job duties with ease. In addition, the benefits that exercise has on productivity extends beyond the workplace. You will feel less tired after your shift ends, leaving you with more willpower to clean your home, socialize, or spend time on a hobby.

Exercising on a regular basis is one of the simplest methods of increasing productivity. According to research, twenty to thirty minutes of vigorous physical activity will significantly benefit one's health. Thankfully, you can work bits of exercise into your daily routine. For example, if you have the choice, climb a staircase instead of riding an elevator. If it is reasonable to do so, walk to your destinations instead of driving or commuting. Even when I drive I constantly park far away from the entry of the supermarket for the same. Actually, I park in the farthest lot so I get to walk from and to my car when I do my groceries. If your job allows it, check emails from your smartphone while you stroll about your workplace's neighborhood. Anything that you can do to cut out idle periods of non-movement will benefit you greatly in the long run.

Take Breaks the Right Way

Taking a break from working can breed several incredible benefits. While a break may seem like an unproductive use of time, its proven benefits will lead to higher levels of productivity upon returning to work. Science suggests that breaks increase energy, raise willpower, and reduce levels of stress. A break can give you the motivation boost that you need to power through your large task. However, not all breaks are created equal. Follow the suggestions in this section to get the most out of your breaks.

First, do not work while you take a break. This seems obvious, but you would be surprised at how many people try to get work done during their supposed downtime. For example, one might schedule a break from homework, during which they sit on their own couch and watch one of their favorite television programs. However, they might use their smartphone to check emails and schedule group project meetings during this time. A break is meant to refresh and motivate, not serve as a time for working lightly. During your break, turn off any devices that connect you to your to-dos. Of course, keep yourself just accessible enough for somebody to reach you in the case of a true emergency.

Second, get outside. Studies show that the presence of nature has stress-relieving effects. Hike through the forest; stroll down the beach; take a lap around a nearby park. Nature serves to provide us with a less stressful life. Take advantage of the wonders that it has to offer.

Third, move! I know, we already talked about the benefits of exercising but I feel I need to make a strong point: physical movement helps us lower stress levels and feel more motivated. Take advantage of your physiology and perform some physical exercise on your break period. Something as simple as a set of pushups next to your desk will invigorate you and make you feel ready to take on the next project. For further suggestions on workplace exercises, look online for simple calisthenics routines.

Fourth, schedule breaks appropriately. There is no universally correct method for scheduling breaks. Some people might thrive from a twenty minute break every two hours, while others do best with a forty minute break at the end of each four hour interval. In any case, take care to avoid overindulging in breaks. Use them appropriately, and make the most out of them.

Train Your Focus

A lack of focus leads to unproductive work sessions. People have trouble focusing for a variety of perceived reasons. Some individuals cannot stop their mind from wandering. Others lack the patience to see a task through to its completion. Still, many hard-working humans get overwhelmed when they have a large number of items on their to-do list. As a result, they frantically switch their focus between projects as their priorities flip-flop. The unifying theme of these reasons for unfocused work is an inability to stay focused on one single task or scenario. Thankfully, strategies for training one's focus exist. However, if your inability to focus seriously impedes on your quality of life, that may indicate a deeper underlying problem. If you believe that your poor focus requires help beyond that which the pages of this book can offer, consult with a mental health professional. Otherwise, read on for suggestions concerning how you can improve your ability to focus.

First, take up reading for pleasure. Reading stories, articles, and other publications will lead to an increase in focusing abilities. Not only do you have to concentrate on the printed words in order to make sense of a publication, you also have to follow the author's train of thought. The best authors make that easy. Try to spend thirty minutes a day reading through a single publication. Books, newspapers, and various publications make great tools for training one's focus because they do not allow consumers to switch their focus to another stimulus. Television allows viewers to choose a different channel. You can still consume video content while you are occupied with another task. Printed words require that you devote the near entirety of your attention to them in order to make sense of and consume them.

Second, practice mindfulness meditation. This type of meditation involves focusing on one single aspect of the human body or surrounding environment, such as one's own breathing pattern or the sound coming from the building's furnace. By making a practice of intently directing your focus to something that otherwise would have not entered your conscious awareness, you stand to go through life with increased levels of awareness and focus.

To engage in mindfulness mediation, find a comfortable seat that you can stay in for the duration of your practice. You can lie down if you wish, but you may drift off. The goal of mindfulness meditation is not to fall asleep.

Next, close your eyes. Your vision will distract you from the stimulus of your focus. Make a point to sit comfortably without opening your eyes.

Finally, focus in on your chosen stimulus. One of the simplest and most effective methods of mindfulness meditation involves focusing on the sensations of one's own breathing. Notice the air flowing in and out of your nostrils. Feel the rising and dropping of your midsection as you inhale and breathe out. If your mind starts to wander, notice and ackowledge the thoughts as they come, and then resume focusing on your breath. Wandering thoughts are perfectly okay; the practice involves actively noticing and becoming aware of when those distracting thoughts enter your head. Start over as many times as you need to and do not get frustrated with yourself if you find that you have a hard time staying focused on breathing. Patience and a willingness to improve are essential for mindfulness meditation's effectiveness.

The practice of mindfulness meditation has many benefits beyond an improved ability to focus. In fact, at least one branch of the United States' military is experimenting with the practice as an effective method for lowering the stress levels of troops. Research suggests that mindfulness meditation causes a drop in its practitioners' cortisol levels. In addition, mindfulness meditation has been shown to ease the effects of the common cold, reduce depression levels, cause a drop in feelings of loneliness, increase compassion, regulate emotions, boost self-awareness, make music sound more dynamic, prevent mental illnesses, and promote better sleep for those who practice it regularly.

Green Tea

Green tea contains a helpful antioxidant that improves mental performance. Catechins, a substance found in green tea, improves memory, focus, and attention while reducing cognitive dysfunction. Drink green tea to improve your performances at work and school.

Here's a lesser known and somewhat surprising fact of green tea: it works just the opposite of coffee or black tea. If you make your tea strong it will make you sleepy but if you make it light it will refresh and invigorate you! To fully experience what this wonderful treasure of nature can do for you try this for a week: drink a large mug of light green tea instead of your morning coffee and try drinking the same size but stronger in the evening in about an hour or two before your bedtime. Within a few days, you will start feeling the difference! It will help you get your morning started with a lot of healthy energy, balance you out during your day and aid you in getting a good night's sleep.

Listen to Your Body

Working hard, even when you do not feel like doing so, will breed results. However, sometimes you just need to take time off. Serious illnesses, mental breakdowns, and extreme fatigue must be rectified before getting back to the grind. If you find yourself in desperate need of rest or help, it is perfectly okay and even encouraged to abandon your day job and schoolwork until you get better. Nothing will halt your productivity more than an unattended debilitating issue.

So, for example, if you wake up with a fever while covered in cold sweat, take the day off and find out what you need to do to get better. If that means staying in bed for three days to rest, then so be it. Never jeopardize your long-term wellbeing in exchange for a few days of sluggish progress. Money, status, and power mean nothing if you are not well enough to enjoy them. If your body is desperately telling you to slow down, you should listen to it. Success should not come at the expense of your sanity and health.

Chapter 4: What Not to Do

Productively accomplishing feats is just as much a matter of avoiding mistakes as it is doing the right things. The sections in this chapter will list errors that contribute to underachieving, as well as hints regarding how to avoid making them. Just dropping one or two of the following bad behaviors will breed immense benefits for you and your productivity levels.

Multitasking

Study after study shows that multitasking is not an efficient method for accomplishing tasks. Still, countless people swear that they are the exception to those findings. The truth is, however, when you try to pay attention to several things at once, you lose focus. Multitaskers cannot efficiently move from one task to another. They often feel overwhelmed as they take on several tasks at once. When you get the urge to multitask, ask yourself if completing projects one at a time would be any less efficient. Chances are very high that you will have an easier, more efficient work session if you avoid multitasking.

On the other hand, multitasking makes itself appropriate in very specific situations. For example, you might make your bed and do the dishes while you wait for your washing machine to finish washing your laundry. In this case, the machine does the bulk of the work for you, allowing you to dedicate almost the entirety of your focus to other tasks. Consider multitasking only in situations where one task allows you to idly stand by for most of it.

Idly Staring at Screens

So many people throw their valuable time away by idly staring at screens. Video games, television, online video content, and movies are some of the modern world's biggest time wasters. Do not use your time consuming these entertaining time wasters. Studies find that the average adult in America watches somewhere close to four hours of television programming every day. Can you believe that? One sixth of the average American adult's day goes to waste.

Make better use of your time. Do not be average. Get yourself off of the sofa and be productive. Many people turn to television after work because they believe that they spent some time working hard, so they must be "done" for the day. You are done when you are dead. Instead of letting screens consume the entirety of your focus, use that time to finish nagging tasks like cleaning and tidying. Better yet, work on something that you care about. There is nothing wrong with working to pay the bills; that is what most adults do. However, it is all too easy to come home, indulge in your intoxicant of choice, and get lost in Netflix until bedtime. I will never understand why some people choose to throw their time away watching television and playing video games purely for entertainment.

Of course, if your job or hobby dictates that you consume screen-based entertainment, then go right ahead. For example, an independent professional wrestler will want to watch WWE programming at every opportunity to get a sense of what audiences react to and to study wrestling psychology. However, in most cases, you will achieve more if you ditch the television. Not only are satellite, cable, and video content subscriptions a waste of time, they also cost money. Quit making yourself unproductive. Move any centrally located televisions in your home to a less accessible area. Better yet, sell them off. You may struggle to find something to do in the evenings at first, but your future self will thank you as you use that time more productively.

Web Browsing

If you work in a modern office, chances are you have access to the internet. Unfortunately, the internet provides a source of limitless distractions. Many people reduce their productivity levels by indulging in web browsing throughout the day. Aimless social media use, video viewing, and content reading contributes nothing to your potential accomplishments. If, while working, you come across internet content that you absolutely must look at, write that content's information down so that you can search for and find it during your free time. Web browsing is one of the biggest time wasters in contemporary workplaces. If you have trouble with web-based distractions, install software that will prevent you from accessing it and have a trusted friend set its password.

Snoozing

Using the snooze button in an attempt to obtain an extra few minutes of sleep is actually counterproductive. Not only do you lose out on valuable time that could have been spent out of bed, you also make it harder on yourself to become alert after waking. When humans first wake up, their body starts producing hormones that contribute to the alertness that is required of a waking state. When you go back to sleep for a few minutes, you do not get the kind of sleep that replenishes your energy. Instead, you slow down the production of alertness hormones, making it more difficult for you to fully awaken and start your day.

You are better off waking up and sacrificing ten minutes of rest than you are using a snooze button.

Too Much Perspective

Perspective is a great thing. If you can see the bigger picture, then you will go far in life. However, a grand perspective can distract one's focus from the task at hand. If you think about planning your whole life after college while you are typing out a paper, then you will not be able to devote as much focus as you could to your paper. Have a plan in mind, but take your life one task at a time. Focusing too much on the ultimate goal can leave you overwhelmed and stressed. In addition, you may feel like you are falling behind on your progress towards that ultimate goal as you spend time grinding out assignments and projects. However, nothing worth having was ever attained without effort. Every task that you complete puts you one step closer to your dream accomplishment. Stay focused and in the moment. Your time will come.

Rewarding Yourself with Cheating

Many people like to cheat themselves as a reward. For example, a person devoted to their diet may reward their own healthy eating habits with a donut. Not only is this highly unproductive, it also trains you to desire the things that you wish to avoid. Cheating for a reward defeats the purpose of your goal. If you treat the thing that you need to avoid like some kind of forbidden fruit, then you will struggle to resist that thing. For example, some people who dedicate themselves to budget better might reward their own frugality by "cheating" their budget and spending money on a new pair of shoes that they do not need. A recovering alcoholic should not reward their own abstinence with a beer. Likewise, do not reward your productivity with a day of unproductivity. Doing so might encourage you to give up on your goals entirely, since you already strayed from the path of productivity anyways. Stay disciplined, and never think of the opportunity to behave badly as a reward for good behavior.

Too Many Meetings

Meetings require attendees to take precious time out of their day in order to attend. That time could be better spent on finishing tasks around the office. Keep meetings to a minimum. If you can avoid attending one, you should probably try to. Sometimes, you can get out of a meeting by shutting yourself in your office. Of course, if you will face discipline or miss out on valuable information that directly relates to your job, then you should attend.

If you must get in touch with several people at once, see if you can host that meeting through digitally mediated platform like a conference call. Digitally mediated meetings allow people to attend from a location of their own choosing. Any meetings that you do attend or host should adhere to an agenda in order to maximize their efficiency.

Passing Time

So many people waste hours while simultaneously convincing themselves that they are working efficiently. I once watched a friend of mine play video games for twenty minutes while he waited for his girlfriend to arrive at the apartment. I made an off-handed comment about how he was wasting time. He responded with "I am passing time." I shut my mouth in disbelief and walked off. Maybe it just bothered me that he would idly stare at a screen while he had dirty dishes in our sink, but I was genuinely bewildered at how anyone could think that "passing time" is a good way to use time.

Make use of the time that you would otherwise spend waiting. For example, you can probably make your bed in the time that it takes your microwave to thaw out your frozen food. Get some reading done while you wait for your laundry to finish. Never simply "pass time." That is a waste. Instead, make the most out of your waiting periods and use them productively. The next time you put a dish to bake in the oven, see if you can finish something else before it finishes cooking.

Still on the same note, here is a rather deep though stemming from an interesting question:

why our last moments of life seem so precious yet we tend to waste our life on a daily basis like we live forever? This is a philosophical dilemma. On a deathbed, most people would give everything for a few extra minutes of life yet when not faced our mortality we piss away our minutes, hours days, weeks even years! Would you still be playing Call of Duty if you knew you had only 60 minutes to live? Would you still be channel surfing if you were aware that you had about an hour left of your life? I know this thought addresses not just wasting time but multiple issues like treating people with love and respect. Either way, there is unfathomable wisdom in it so spend every moment like it is your last!

Procrastinating

Similar to passing time, procrastinating involves intentionally putting off important tasks. Needless to say, this is a huge waste of time. People procrastinate for a variety of reasons, including fear of failure, fear of success, lack of interest, lack of motivation, lack of knowledge, and a desire for resistance.

First, fear of failure causes many individuals to procrastinate, even on pressing projects. Trying hard only to fail can lead to disappointment and a reduction in the confidence that one has for themselves. As a result, people try to protect their egos by avoiding tasks that they may not succeed at. In their minds, not trying equates to not truly failing. If you never try, then you can tell yourself that your results are not a true reflection of your abilities. For example, say that you procrastinate on an essay for one of your classes. You work hard on it for a few hours the night before it is due, but you pay no attention to it otherwise. Consequently, you receive a mediocre grade. You then have the luxury of telling yourself something to the effect of "I only got a low grade because I waited so long to get started. If I had more time to finish, I could have earned a much higher grade." If you can lose your ego, humble yourself, and diligently work on your assignments, you stand to improve your performance and avoid procrastinating.

Conversely, fear of success causes some people to procrastinate hard. You might avoid putting much time into a project because you fear that your boss will hold you to that same standard once he or she realizes your capabilities. Furthermore, an outstanding performance may bring unwanted attention onto yourself. This kind of procrastination often happens when people link their self-worth to their accomplishments, either subconsciously or consciously.

Next, a lack of interest plays a huge role in explaining why some people tend to procrastinate. Finding a subject or work assignment boring on occasion is normal. However, using the lack of interest as a reason to procrastinate is not acceptable. Instead, you should just tackle boring responsibilities as soon as they arise. You have the opportunity to achieve a lot if you humble yourself and clinch your teeth. When you put your head down and finish such undesirable tasks in a timely manner, you will enjoy your free time a lot more. Getting boring things done will allow you to relax without worrying about unfinished assignments.

Fourth, some procrastinators get into the habit of procrastinating because they lack motivation. In other words, they will avoid doing something simply because they have no desire to do it. I have no patience for these types of people. Not wanting to do something is not an excuse for not doing it. You cannot sit around and wait for motivation to strike. Instead, you have to accept that you have a responsibility to handle, and then get to work. Experts in productivity suggest that you will feel motivated to finish an undesirable task only once you start working on it. The rewarding feeling that you get from your progress and accomplishments will further motivate you to achieve more as you continue to chase that rewarding feeling.

Fifth, many procrastinators put off work because they have no knowledge of the subject of their delayed project. For example, a person who knows nothing about cars might procrastinate on getting their oil changed out of fear of saying something that makes them look ignorant to the mechanic. For others, the research required to properly begin the task in question is enough to make them not want to start any time soon. As another example, some people who type very slowly may delay doing work on an essay for school. The tedious work that typing an essay requires of them makes them fear projects that require large amounts of typing. The slow progress that they make on such projects makes them feel incapable and lacking in skills. However, everybody has something that they are not any good at. Better yet, typing a lengthy essay is a great way to improve one's typing speed. Still, lack of knowledge causes people to procrastinate and avoid improving their unimpressive skills.

Finally, angst can cause some egotistical individuals to procrastinate. These types of people go through life with the attitude that they can have everything that they desire without ever working hard. The cause of this attitude stems from the fact that somebody whom the procrastinator despises tried to make them work on a task. For example, maybe a student despises how his father constantly pushed him to stay on top of his schoolwork. As a result, the young student would avoid doing schoolwork in order to rebel against his father's wishes. Unfortunately, this type of behavior is highly reactionary. It is not proactive. Those who procrastinate out of resistance or angst are reacting to the expectations that others have of them. Ultimately, if you procrastinate for this reason, you are turning over control of your accomplishments to the very person that you wish to rebel against.

The solutions to procrastination will vary according to its causes. However, most cases of procrastination can be overcome if one only accepts their suffering, gets up, and gets to work. Humility and work ethic can overcome nearly every desire to procrastinate.

Making Excuses

Excuses kill ambition. People will find any excuse to absolve themselves of responsibility for their shortcomings. The world may very well be stacked against you. However, making such excuses will not get you any farther in life. Take responsibility for any failures you experience. When you make excuses, you place the power to rectify the scenario into the hands of the person or thing that you blame.

For example, maybe you were late to the office this morning. You can blame traffic, sure. That would make traffic responsible for your tardiness, and thus eliminate any perceived need to make adjustments to your commuting process. However, you cannot control the traffic. You can, however, control the time at which you get on the road in the morning, so you can ensure your timeliness in the future by planning to leave your home earlier next time. Instead of blaming an external force for your deficiencies, ask yourself what you could have done differently. You can control your own behavior and actions, so give power to them. Accept responsibility for your own shortcomings and successes. Blaming that which you have no control over makes you ultimately powerless.

Similarly, some people will dig for excuses to remain unproductive. For example, a student might tell himself that he cannot do his homework because he is too tired, thanks to the assignment that he stayed up late finishing last night, only to spend the afternoon watching movies. In this scenario, the student gives power to his other coursework, citing it as the reason for his unproductivity. In his mind, he has the right to idly stare at a screen because he worked hard the night before. Sadly, he sacrifices any control he had over the situation. Instead of watching movies, he could have spent a few hours catching up on sleep, and then woke up rejuvenated and ready to get to work. Do not let outside forces serve as an excuse for wasting time. Successful individuals do not say that they do not have time; instead, they make the most of their time.

Furthermore, some people let their perceived lack of ability serve as an excuse for not even trying. They tell themselves that they do not have the skills to perform a certain task, so they might as well not even bother with making an honest effort. However, skills can be improved. If you believe that you lack the skills to get what you want in life, keep practicing and bettering yourself until you reach the level of ability that inspires confidence within yourself. Self-loathing should never serve as an excuse for inaction.

Avoiding Discomfort

Many people who otherwise work hard never reach their true potential because they would rather stay comfortable. In other words, complacency ruins productivity. If productivity is the key to success in life, then complacency is productivity's kryptonite. A working person might want to get a better job, but the effort required to get a college degree deters them from pursuing the education needed to obtain exclusive positions. Ask yourself, would you rather work hard for a few years, or live a whole life of mediocrity? Many unfortunate beings with unlimited potential squander it on comfortability.

Watching videos on the couch in the evenings is, indisputably, an unproductive use of time. Still, countless people choose to do just that because it is immediately comfortable.

Listening to the Haters

Any time that you try to accomplish something great, there will be somebody who wants to see you fail. Commonly referred to as "haters," these naysayers will go out of their way to make you doubt yourself. Haters get that way because of jealousy. They are jealous of your drive. They are jealous of your potential success. They wish that they could be as productive as you are, so they try to make you give up instead of focusing on improving their own lives.

That jealousy can quickly turn to hate. The best thing that you can do in a situation involving a hater is ignore them. Take a look at your doubter's work ethic. Chances are, it does not come close to matching yours.

Truthfully, some haters actually hate themselves so much that they have to redirect their hatred towards someone other than themselves. Carefully directed hatred can give a hater a sense of self-righteous indignation. These are the same people who will watch a television show that they do not enjoy just to critique its writing from their own sofa. If you start making some serious accomplishments in life, you may find yourself with a large group of haters trying to stop you from achieving. For example, many prominent musicians and politicians have haters in large numbers. Some even go so far as to write blogs, news articles, and social media posts disparaging these public figures. Instead of showing happiness and adopting a congratulatory attitude towards another person's success, they badmouth that person and attempt to hurt their reputation.

When faced with a hater, recognize that their attitude is likely a reflection of their own shortcomings and insecurities. Do not entertain the idea that you might be wrong because you took it upon yourself to make achievements in life. Once another person has decided, usually subconsciously, to act as a hater, do not try to reason with them. Once it reaches a decision, especially one fueled by emotions like hatred, the human mind tends to resist information that contradicts its beliefs. Haters selectively attend to the evidence that supports their hateful beliefs, so you will have a hard time reasoning with them. Ignore them and keep achieving. With enough effort, you just might make a believer out of them (although that should not be the primary focus of your endeavors).

Judging Others

There is nothing wrong with engaging in self-criticism. In fact, self-criticism, when executed right, can make a great tool for self-assessment. However, when you find yourself silently criticizing others, you face a whole gang of issues that will hinder your own performance and productivity.

First, passing judgement on another person is a sign of insecurity. People will make negative assessments about the next person in order to feel better about themselves in comparison. When you silently judge another being, you are likely doing so according to a set of standards that you have been programmed to believe. Sure, the person across from you on the bus may look filthy, but that opinion stems from your standards for cleanliness. Let everybody live life according to their own standards and you will save the mental energy required for diagnosing the problems that other people display. Judging others distracts from your goals. Focus on your own life and work instead.

Chapter 5: Productivity Technology

Technology continues to develop at an unprecedented rate. In fact, many, if not most workplaces in developed nations depend on modern technology as an instrumental part of their operations. The technology described in this chapter will assist readers in using digital platforms to boost their own productivity and achieve more.

Inbox Pause

Inbox Pause is a browser extension that helps users manage their Gmail emails. When installed and activated, Inbox Pause prevents emails from appearing in users' inboxes during the hours of their choosing. These emails go into a separate folder that a user can access at any time. Furthermore, the extension gives users the option to automatically reply to emails that come in at chosen hours. These replies can communicate to senders that the receiver will only check his or her inbox at a certain time and that they can expect to receive a response during those hours. As soon as one chooses to "Unpause" their inbox, all emails received during pausing hours will appear in their inbox as they normally would, had the browser extension not been installed and activated.

IFTTT

IFTTT is a series of applets that help make one's life more productive. Sure, many of the applets save mere seconds, but those seconds add up. For example, you can download one that will cause your garage door to fully open as soon as your car makes its way into your driveway. Another will send any screenshots that you take on your smartphone to your email inbox. Browse IFTTT's website for a more complete idea of the ways that the technology can save you time.

Zapier

Zapier is another smartphone app that automates some of your menial tasks. One such capability makes itself known when the app automatically moves email attachments to your Dropbox. The innovative smartphone app also allows users to transfer information and text between different apps. Consider using Zapier if you find yourself spending too much time organizing digital files and information between apps and programs.

Any.do

This smartphone app gives users the ability to manage all of their errands, tasks, chores, projects, and assignments in one interface. Any.-do acts as a digitized to-do list that promotes increases in productivity. Users can store all of their to-dos and their corresponding dates, times, and deadlines in one app. This app includes a feature that will send a notification to your phone at a predetermined time reminding you to take a look at your upcoming responsibilities. Furthermore, Any.do users can collaborate on to-do lists, encouraging cooperation and teamwork.

Doodle

Large groups often have trouble finding meeting times that work for everyone on the team. Thankfully, Doodle lets collaborators fill out a weekly calendar with times that they are free and the hours in which they are occupied. The program then processes everyone's input to generate a layout of all of the times during which everyone in the group is available to meet. Doodle comes in handy for sudents who get assigned a group project at school, office leaders who need to schedule meetings, and entertainers looking to schedule appropriate rehearsal times.

Dragon NaturallySpeaking

The Dragon NaturallySpeaking software makes itself especially useful for those who type at low speeds. The program allows users to speak into a microphone, at which point the software transcribes the users' speech into written text. It was designed for use with email platforms. More advanced features include the ability to control one's computer's functions with just their voice. Dragon NaturallySpeaking makes itself incredibly useful for those who take the time to learn how to use it. However, its steep price tag and the time required to master its features make it ideal only for those who are serious about increasing their productivity levels.

EasilyDo

The EasilyDo smartphone application increases one's productivity by automating menial, regular tasks that users would otherwise perform manually. For example, you can program the app to post a happy birthday message from your Facebook account to all of your friends' timelines on the appropriate dates. You can also have the app send out a text message to the people who might care when you find yourself running late. EasilyDo's simple setup process and user-friendly design make it an attractive choice for busy people who do not want to take the time to learn difficult, highly technical software and programs.

Google Drive

For those who despise the menial downloading, attaching, and saving that traditionally stored computer files require, Google Drive provides a solution. This program gives users the ability to share, edit, and store files without ever leaving their web browser. You can maneuver files from person to person without them ever making their way onto a hard drive or other form of digital memory. In addition, users can upload files to this program from their computer. Much like computer storage, Google Drive allows users to create folders, rename files, and permanently delete unneeded items. Be warned, however; if you share a file with another Google Drive user, that other user has access to the file until they choose to delete it, even if you delete that same file from your own Google Drive Account.

Google Forms, Sheets, Docs, and Slides

Microsoft Office paved the way for these Google programs. Forms allows users to create and share surveys and receive responses from the people who answer them. Sheets, the illegitimate child of Google and Microsoft Excel, serves the same functions that Excel does. However, Google Sheets do not need to be stored on a hard drive, flash drive, or any other tangible form of computer storage. Instead, all Sheets files are stored on Google's servers, freeing up space on your computer. In addition, users can share these files with one another through the Google interface, eliminating the need for tedious email attachments and sorting files on one's computer. Google Docs and Slides behave the same way, with Docs imitating Microsoft Word and Slides taking the place of PowerPoint. Also, you can access files stored on Google's platform from just about any web browser on any device. Web-based storage and sharing capabilities set these programs apart from their Microsoft Office counterparts.

Inky

Inky is a great program for managing multiple email accounts at once. The program combines all of your inboxes into one consolidated interface.

Carrot

Carrot is a smartphone app that motivates users to accomplish the items listed on their to-do lists. The interface acts as a digital companion. When you finish a task, you earn points that gain you access to higher levels. Upon failing to meet a deadline, an angry face will appear on your screen, scorning you for your lack of productivity. This app combines elements of practicality and silliness to create one of the most fun productivity apps on the market.

Chapter 6: Prepare for Tomorrow

A more productive life leads to lower levels of stress. As you cross items off of your to-do list, you will feel the ease that comes along with knowing that you have fewer obligations ahead of you. Preparation never hurt anyone. Save yourself worry and hurry tomorrow by doing a bit of preparation today.

Make Meals in Bulk

Home cooking, while an economical and healthy way of obtaining nourishment, can eat up a large portion of one's time. Navigate this problem by preparing your meals in bulk. You can then heat up leftovers throughout the week. For example, you can cook two pounds of ground turkey for yourself at one time. Then, you only need to add the meat to a tortilla, heat it up, and add some cheese and veggies for a quick burrito.

Pack Your Bag

For most busy people, a bag is an essential part of one's wardrobe. Students carry backpacks; office workers tote briefcases; manual laborers carry toolboxes and safety gear; performing artists travel with suitcases that contain their costumes.

You stand to save yourself a lot of effort in the future if you pack your bag on the day before you need to carry it.

Packing in advance comes in handy when you have unknowingly misplaced one or more of your bag's essential contents. If you need to look for something, packing the night before gives you plenty of time to find it. Advance packing will prevent you from scrambling about your dwelling as you desperately try to find what you need and still make it to wherever you are headed on time.

Furthermore, packing for tomorrow will reduce the likelihood that you forget an item. As you prepare your bag, you will mentally go through the things that need to go into that bag. You will have an entire night to remember anything that you might have forgotten to include. On the other hand, packing a bag immediately before going out the door with it does not leave you much time to consider whether you remembered everything. Packing a bag right before you need it makes you more likely to forget to pack something. Save yourself a lot of time and trouble by preparing your bag one day in advance.

Pick Your Clothes

Avoid wasting time in the mornings as you hurriedly decide on which outfit combination suits you best. Instead, calmly choose the next day's clothing before you go to bed. Check the weather and plan your garments accordingly. In addition, this time-saving practice will prevent you from rushing to find lost articles of clothing. You would hate to be late to work all because you could not find a tie to go with your jacket.

Pack Your Lunch

Save even more time and stress during your morning routine by packing yourself a lunch the night before. You will thank yourself as you have access to a fully prepared, healthy meal of your choosing the next day. In addition, you can carefully pick every ingredient that makes its way into your home-prepared lunches. Fast foods do not give diners such choices. As such, follow the suggestions found in the healthy eating section in chapter 3 for optimal lunch preparation.

Set Timers

Automated timers add a helpful element of convenience to the working person's routine. Make use of them and you will hardly ever find yourself struggling for time because you forgot to do some task. For example, if you enjoy a serving of coffee in the mornings, get yourself a coffee maker with a settable timer that will start brewing coffee at a designated time, ideally a few minutes after you wake up. Timers will make your life easier and more convenient.

Arrange Transportation

How do you plan on getting to work or school in the morning? If you ride a public bus, plan your route and departure time to allow for delays. Bus drivers are only human, and, despite how hard they try, they sometimes fall behind on their route. Allow yourself an extra fifteen to twenty minutes to arrive at your destination. If you arrive early, make the most of that extra time and do something productive.

If you drive a vehicle of your own, stay updated on traffic conditions and potential road closures. Driving on public roads lends itself to unpredictable delays. Plan to allow yourself more than enough time to arrive safely.

Walking perhaps gives us the most control over our arrival time. Traffic accidents and road conditions will rarely delay a walker. A walker will not be delayed if a bus shows up late. If you live in an area with unpredictable traffic patterns and unreliable public transportation, consider walking if the distance seems reasonable.

Preview Your Work Week on Sunday

As the weekend comes to an end, most of us try to avoid the inevitable workday that soon follows. As such, many working people spend their Sundays trying their hardest to avoid thinking about work. Unfortunately, this leads to a stressful Monday, as the transition from a highly slothful weekend often makes itself abrupt. Spend a small amount of time during your Sunday evenings previewing the work week to come. If you are a student, take a peek at the syllabi that your professors gave you. If you are a working professional, go over any appointments, meetings, and deadlines that you expect to face in the coming week. By giving yourself a brief preview, you can better plan your time to work around scheduled obligations.

Prepare for Emergencies

Unfortunately, unpredictable emergencies can happen at any time. A natural disaster or medical condition can put a halt to one's daily routine. As such, it is important to prepare for the unexpected. Stock up on emergency supplies. If you live in a rural or isolated community, you will want to have a bigger stockpile than someone who lives in a busy metropolis. Larger cities have more access to resources.

Of course, you should attend to urgent emergencies as they arise, which may mean taking a break from work or school in order to handle a crisis. Success, fame, and wealth should not be prioritized above personal safety. Emergency circumstances really do lie beyond any one person's control. In the event of an emergency, tend to yourself and your loved ones before your career. At the end of the day, your bank balance is just a number that should not determine your self-worth. Safety and wellbeing should come before any paycheck, publicity, or promotion.

Conclusion

Thank you for making it through to the end of *Smarter Faster Better: Work Smarter, Not Harder*. I hope that readers find it informative and able to provide them with all of the tools that they need to accomplish their productivity goals, whatever those may be.

The next step is to take the advice found within this book's pages and apply it wherever possible. In the preceding pages, we covered ways to maximize output, complete tasks in less time, enhance one's own ability to perform, navigate potential hindrances, make use of productivity technology, and prep for the future. This book can only show you how; the responsibility to take action lies in your hands.

Dear Reader,

if you are a traditional eater and interested in how you can max out your health potential just by developing proper eating habits consider reading my other book Eatin Clean! This nutritional strategy helped me to get going on my still ongoing journey towards getting into and staying in the best shape of my life!

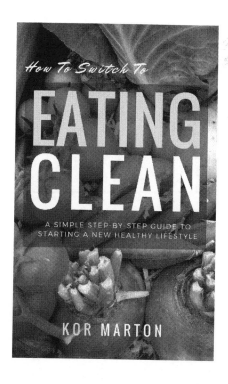

Please visit my website, be my friend on Facebook, follow me on Twitter and subscribe to me on Youtube!

http://www.passiveincomemillionaire.pro/
https://www.facebook.com/PassiveIncomeMillionaire/
https://twitter.com/KorMarton

Finally, if you found this book useful in anyway, a review on Amazon is always appreciated!

Planetkor Publishing
18375 Ventura Blvd #379
Tarzana, CA 91356

www.planetkor.com
Kor@planetkor.com

First Edition

91647197R00064

Made in the USA
Middletown, DE
01 October 2018